ROLL UP, ROLL UP!

Based on the 1941 Walt Disney animation, *Dumbo* brings one of the studio's most beloved characters to vivid life in an all-new, live-action adventure, directed by the visionary Tim Burton (*Edward Scissorhands*, *Alice in Wonderland*).

From the appealingly shabby hucksterism of the Medici Brothers Circus, to the awe-inspiring spectacle of Coney Island's Dreamland, *Dumbo* takes you on a fantastical journey through the circus worlds of 1919, while using state-of-the-art visual effects to make its main character feel as real as his human co-stars.

It is a movie that will truly make you believe an elephant can fly.

COLLECT THE OFFICIAL DISNEY SPECIALS

Dumbo
Toy Story 4
Artemis Fowl
Frozen 2

Editor **Dan Jolin**
Designer **Donna Askem**

TITAN EDITORIAL
Managing Editor **Martin Eden**
Senior Designer **Andrew Leung**
Art Director **Oz Browne**
Senior Production Controller
Jackie Flook
Production Controller **Peter James**
Production Assistant **Rhiannon Roy**
Sales & Circulation Manager
Steve Tothill

Marketing Assistant **Charlie Raspin**
Senior Brand Manager **Chris Thompson**
Senior Publicist **Will O'Mullane**
Ads & Marketing Assistant
Bella Hoy
Commercial Manager
Michelle Fairlamb
Head of Rights **Jenny Boyce**
Publishing Manager **Darryl Tothill**
Publishing Director **Chris Teather**
Operations Director **Leigh Baulch**
Executive Director **Vivian Cheung**
Publisher **Nick Landau**

DISTRIBUTION
US Newsstand: Total Publisher
Services, Inc.
John Dziewiatkowski, 630-851-7683
US Newsstand Distribution:
Curtis Circulation Company
US Bookstore Distribution:
The News Group
US Direct Sales Market:
Diamond Comic Distributors

For more info on advertising contact
adinfo@titanemail.com

ISBN: 9781787731813

Printed in the US by Quad.

Titan Authorized User. No part of this publication
may be reproduced, stored in a retrieval system, or
transmitted, in any form or by any means, without
the prior written permission of the publisher.

DISNEY PUBLISHING WORLDWIDE
Global Magazines, Comics and Partworks
Publisher: Lynn Waggoner.
Editorial Team: Bianca Coletti (Director,
Magazines), Guido Frazzini (Director, Comics),
Stefano Ambrosio (Executive Editor, New IP),
Carlotta Quattrocolo (Executive Editor), Camilla
Vedove (Senior Manager, Editorial Development),
Behnoosh Khalili (Senior Editor), Julie Dorris
(Senior Editor), Mina Riazi (Assistant Editor),
Jonathan Manning (Assistant Editor). Design:
Enrico Soave (Senior Designer). Art: Ken Shue
(VP, Global Art), Roberto Santillo (Creative

Director), Marco Ghiglione (Creative Manager),
Manny Mederos (Senior Illustration Manager),
Stefano Attardi (Computer Art Designer). Portfolio
Management: Olivia Ciancarelli (Director).
Business & Marketing: Mariantonietta Galla
(Marketing Manager), Virpi Korhonen (Editorial
Manager).
Thank you to Christopher Troise, Shiho Tilley,
Eugene Paraszczuk and all at Disney.

A CIP catalogue record for this title is available
from the British Library.

Copyright © 2019 Disney Enterprises, Inc. All
rights reserved.

10 9 8 7 6 5 4 3 2 1

CONTENTS

AN ELEPHANT'S TALE

THE STORY OF ★ DUMBO

When the run-down but plucky Medici Brothers Circus welcomes a new baby elephant to its troupe, they are initially disheartened at its strange, big-eared appearance and name him "Dumbo." But after circus kids Milly and Joe Farrier (Nico Parker and Finley Hobbins) discover Dumbo can use those ungainly ears to fly like a bird, it seems the Medici Brothers Circus' fortunes have changed. Especially when big-time showman V.A. Vandevere (Michael Keaton) offers them all a new home at his vast, New York-based fun palace Dreamland.

Can Vandevere be trusted? Will Dumbo and the Farriers fit into this spectacular new world? And can the kids reunite their magical new friend with his mother, Mrs. Jumbo, who was sent away after a tragic accident? They will need all the help they can get: from haughty aerialist Colette Marchant (Eva Green); to wily ringmaster Max Medici (Danny DeVito); and the Farriers' own father, the damaged but heroic Holt (Colin Farrell).

THE DIRECTOR

THE DIRECTOR

★ TIM BURTON ★

The visionary filmmaker behind *Dumbo* tells Leah Gallo why he was inspired to bring this classic Disney tale to the 21st Century big screen, and how it became a reunion with some dear friends.

Dumbo – The Official Movie Special: **What drove you to make an adaptation of the 1941 animated film *Dumbo*?**

Tim Burton: It's a very sweet story. The idea of a flying elephant is such a simple story. I think that's why it's quite popular and affected people so much, because of how primal and basic it is. I thought the new screenplay offered a way to tell that story in a framework that expanded it, but without redoing the original. It was simple, with an emotional simplicity, and didn't interfere with what the basic throughline of the original is about.

Tell us about the character of Holt Farrier, and why Colin Farrell was the ideal person to play him.

He's war-damaged, he's missing an arm, he used to be a star, he hasn't seen his kids, and he doesn't really know how to deal with his kids or talk to them. To try and do that subtly and emotionally takes a certain type of person – somebody who understands drama and comedy and emotion, all mixed together. It's a subtle part, and those are sometimes the hardest ones to do. Colin's great because he really understood the mixture of all those things. Plus, he can ride a horse, one-armed, and you can't say that about everybody. He was a real collaborator, and really fun to work with.

This is the fourth time you've worked with Danny DeVito. What do you love so much about collaborating with him?
He's an artist and he does lots of different things, and he's interested in lots of different things. He's directed, acted, produced; he's done so much. He's also just a great person to be around – fun and open. He's just the kind of personality everybody really likes. It was great working with him again.

This is also the fourth time you've worked with Michael Keaton — though the last time was back in 1992. How was the reunion?
I hadn't seen him for many years, and it just reminded me of his energy from *Beetlejuice*, that intensity that he has. You don't know whether he's being friendly or wants to kill you. It's really a lot of fun to work with him, and having him and Danny together [they worked together with Burton on *Batman Returns*] – that was great.

Why did you see Eva Green – who previously did *Dark Shadows* and *Miss Peregrine's Home for Peculiar Children* – in the role of aerialist Colette Marchant?
She's the first person I thought of. I could just see her in that role. It's like with all of the cast – I could just see them in the role. She did amazingly with the trapeze work. That's the thing: her dedication to everything is unbelievable. She's got good ideas, and she's a great collaborator. She goes beyond anything.

Alan Arkin is another actor you've worked with before, on *Edward Scissorhands*…

> "The idea of a flying elephant is such a simple story. I think that's why it affected people so much, because of how primal and basic it is."

He's great – a funny guy. I hadn't seen a lot of these people for a long time, so for me it was really nice. I'm talking to Alan, and seeing Danny and Michael Keaton together… That was an amazing feeling for me – all of these people together making great experiences. It's interesting; in some cases, it had been years and years since I'd seen these people, and when I saw and worked with them again, it was like a time machine. You don't feel like any time has gone by.

Dumbo marks the first time you've worked with cinematographer Ben Davis. Why did you choose him?
I met Ben at Longcross [Film Studios, in England] and all the people I'd worked with have spoken very highly of him. I didn't know his work very well, and then I just met him and liked him – that's obviously a big part of the collaboration. Then I saw some of his work and he just dealt with a lot of variables. He'd done independent films, and big and small ones. It's nice to work with people who are good and creative, but who you also like to be around, because you're around these people – camera and everybody – all day, so it's nice to have a positive, creative energy like Ben's. ▶

01 Burton directs Colin Farrell as returning World War I soldier Holt Farrier.

02 Burton shares a joke with Danny DeVito (Max Medici), Alan Arkin (J. Griffin Remington) and Michael Keaton (V.A. Vandevere).

03 Burton with regular collaborator Eva Green, who plays celebrated aerialist Colette Marchant.

Many different methods were used to represent Dumbo on set. How did you find that experience?

From the outside it must have looked a bit ridiculous and absurd. What will be pulled out for this scene? Edd [Osmond, who performs Dumbo]? The stuffie? The wire version of an elephant? Every shot had its own problem and how to deal with it. So we just took each shot as it came and blended in different techniques that worked best for each.

Why was it so important to build so many extensive sets, rather than generate your environments using green screen and visual effects?

It helps when you have sets rather than complete green screen/blue screen movies. That's hard. There is something to be said for feeling at least part of the environment. Working at Cardington Studios [the former airship hangar in Bedfordshire, England] was like being in a giant toolshed. It was good. I don't know where else we could have built Dreamland. The scale was right and it was a good space to build in.

04 Burton the ringmaster, on the Medici Brothers Circus set with Farrell and Parker.

05 Burton shows newcomer Nico Parker (Milly Farrier) the way in an upcoming scene.

06 Burton gives Finley Hobbins (Joe Farrier) some notes.

07 *Dumbo* marks the first time Burton and Farrell have worked together.

> "The circus is a place for everybody that doesn't fit into any category. It means going to hook up with a bunch of weirdos, whatever race or gender."

Circuses, and circus themes, appear in a lot of your movies. What fascinates you so much about them?

There are mixtures of every different kind of person. It's that whole thing about running away to the circus. I never particularly wanted to, but it's an idea. You don't fit in, so you're going away to a place where other people don't fit in. I think that's what the circus represents on a positive level. It's a place for everybody that doesn't fit into any category. It means going to hook up with a bunch of other weirdos, whatever race or gender. It's also cool to be surrounded by all of these weirdly talented people. 🎬

06

07

THE IDEAL SHOWMAN

FILM EXPERT IAN FREER OFFERS FIVE REASONS WHY TIM BURTON IS THE PERFECT CHOICE TO DIRECT *DUMBO*.

1. HE UNDERSTANDS OUTSIDERS

When Dumbo is introduced to the circus crowd and his abnormally large ears are revealed, the public turn on him and boo. In that moment, he becomes a true Tim Burton hero. From his early films like *Edward Scissorhands* to more recent offerings such as *Miss Peregrine's Home for Peculiar Children*, Burton has long been drawn to those sidelined by society, taking characters who might be traditionally deemed weird and treating them with empathy. At its heart, *Dumbo* revels in the simple idea that drives many of Burton's movies: what makes you different also makes you special.

2. DISNEY IS IN HIS DNA

Burton started out as an animator at Walt Disney Studios, where he worked on features *The Fox and the Hound* and *The Black Cauldron* and made two short films: *Vincent* and *Frankenweenie* (the latter remade by Burton as a full-length feature in 2012). Years later, he returned to the studio to make *Alice in Wonderland*, which not only became his biggest hit to date, grossing more than $1 billion, but also kickstarted the trend for live-action Disney adaptations. In many ways, returning to reimagine *Dumbo*, based on the 1941 animated classic, is a homecoming.

3. HE FINDS FAMILY IN UNLIKELY PLACES

As much as it celebrates individuality, *Dumbo* is also a story that thrives on the joy of discovering family and friendship in unlikely places. The idea of unconventional families courses through Burton's work. *Miss Peregrine's Home for Peculiar Children* depicts a warm and welcoming refuge for kids who have been shunned by the outside world. And the filmmaking troupe of *Ed Wood*, a band of oddballs gathered around the famously terrible movie director, may be strange, but together they form a supportive network.

4. HE HAS A UNIQUE SENSE OF STYLE

No one else makes films like Tim Burton. His movies are a distinctive mix of the childlike and the grownup, of fantasy and reality, all topped off with genuinely earned emotion. Burton has a real feel for bringing fairy tales to the big screen. In films such as *Edward Scissorhands*, *Sleepy Hollow* and particularly *Alice in Wonderland*, he creates worlds of fairy dust and dreamscapes, simple but elegantly told fables filled with magic – sometimes enchanting, sometimes dark – that transport the audience to a different time or place. *Dumbo*, with its lamp-lit glow, continues this idea of making movies that look like a children's storybook.

5. HE MAKES FILMS ON THE BIGGEST SCALE

Burton is a master showman, orchestrating grand set pieces on a huge canvas. He delivered a full-scale alien invasion in *Mars Attacks!* and brought Roald Dahl's *Charlie and the Chocolate Factory* to vivid life. He has always been at the cutting edge of visual-effects technology. In 1988's *Beetlejuice*, he combined makeup, puppetry, miniature models and stop-motion animation techniques to create a zany view of the afterlife. Burton entered the digital world in a big way with 2010's *Alice in Wonderland*, which featured an impressive 2,300 VFX shots. *Dumbo* continues this tradition. With its beloved lead character realized entirely through astonishingly photo-real digital effects, and all its extravagant environments built on studio soundstages, it is Burton's most ambitious movie yet.

Concept art depicting Dumbo's firefighting clown routine. Production designer Rick Heinrichs describes it as "an important element we've preserved from the original film," although he used a real-life Coney Island spectacle as inspiration, too.

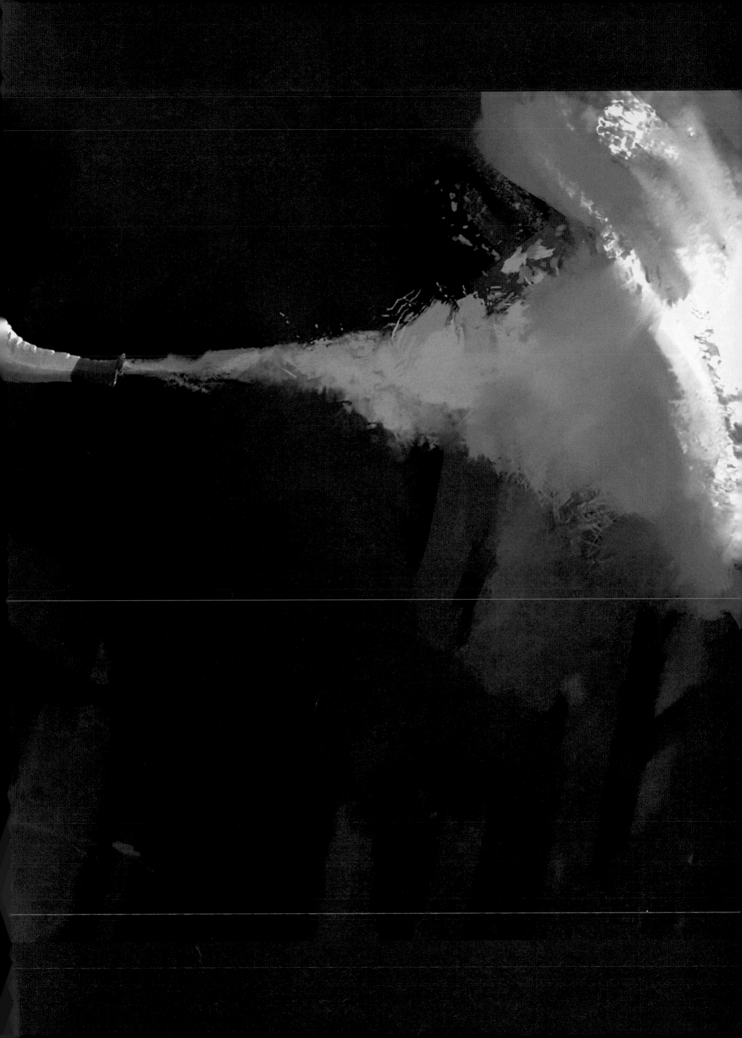

COLIN FARRELL

IS

★ HOLT FARRIER ★

In director Tim Burton's reimagining of animated classic *Dumbo*, Colin Farrell stars as Holt Farrier, a wounded war hero and former circus rider tasked with looking after a strange baby elephant, as well as his own two children... Here, Farrell reveals what it's like being part of Burton's flying-elephant circus.

02

Dumbo – The Official Movie Special:
Why did you want to be part of this film?
Colin Farrell: Tim Burton, more than anything. I've been a fan of Tim's for 20 years – *Edward Scissorhands* was the first film of his I saw. When I heard he was doing *Dumbo*, it seemed like such a beautiful marriage of magical, fantastical material and a director who's so renowned for his incredible imagination and artistic virtue. It was a no-brainer.

Who is Holt Farrier?

He was half of a double act with his wife, before he went off to fight in the First World War. They had a horse act where they would do roping tricks and trick riding, but he was sent off to fight and left his wife and two children behind. By the time he comes back, his wife has passed away and his children have been raised by the circus. He's also lost his left arm in battle, so he is both physically and psychologically wounded. He comes back to a life that he doesn't recognize. He doesn't know how to deal with the grief of having lost his wife.

What place does Holt find in the circus?

He becomes the elephant trainer without any background experience. It's humiliating and humbling for him. He's just shoveling elephant poop, until this baby elephant is born, with a somewhat displeasing set of ears to all who look upon it for the first time. Medici (Danny DeVito),

01 Colin Farrell as Holt Farrier with Eva Green as Colette Marchant.

02 Farrell as Holt Farrier, with his circus-raised children Milly (Nico Parker) and Joe (Finley Hobbins).

03 Concept art depicts Holt Farrier's return from World War I – a difficult reunion with his children, Milly and Joe.

04 To play one-time stunt rider Holt, Farrell had to undergo rigorous horse training.

> "*Dumbo* is such a beautiful marriage of magical material and a director who's so renowned for his incredible imagination."

who's the ringmaster and the owner of the circus, thinks it's going to sink his circus, until Holt's kids find out the elephant somehow has the power of flight.

What was it like working with Tim Burton?

An absolute joy. He really is so intuitive. Obviously, the story is imbued with an incredible sweetness – there's this pervasive sweetness and sense of hope and playfulness to the whole thing. It could dip into the realm of being too sickly sweet, but Tim is constantly looking to pull it back. He has a high regard for the audience and doesn't want to beat them over the head with the sweetness of the film. Having said all that, he has designed these incredible worlds, and the sets I was on daily were like nothing I've ever seen. They're so beautiful and so evocative, and if you have any sense of a child inside you, that's provoked as soon as you walk on set. Tim's incredibly engaged in the whole storytelling process. He's feeling and breathing and thinking his way through everything the characters are going through on-screen. He's just extraordinary to watch.

03

04

FARRELL TRIVIA

FIVE THINGS YOU DIDN'T KNOW ABOUT COLIN FARRELL

1. His father and uncle, Eamon and Tommy, were professional soccer players, who both played for the Shamrock Rovers in Ireland during the late 1950s and '60s.

2. When Farrell was 17 years old, he auditioned to be a member of '90s Irish boyband Boyzone, but by his own admission did terribly. He had to sing George Michael's "Careless Whisper" twice – apparently, he was asked to perform it again because the first attempt was so bad.

3. In 1997, just a year before his acting career took off, Farrell worked as a line-dancing instructor in a nightclub in Limerick, Ireland.

4. He dropped out of Dublin's Gaiety Drama School in 1998, but auditioned for the role of Danny Byrne in British TV hit *Ballykissangel* just a month later. He got the part, which kick-started his career.

5. He and Johnny Depp have both played the same role in a movie on two different occasions: Tony, in 2009's *The Imaginarium of Doctor Parnassus* (which was also shared with Jude Law and Heath Ledger), and Graves, aka Grindlewald, in 2017's *Fantastic Beasts and Where to Find Them*.

What was it like being on the set of Dreamland, the theme park built by Michael Keaton's character, V.A. Vandevere?

In 20 years I've seen some beautiful sets. On *Total Recall*, they had some extraordinary sets. On *Alexander*, we had some amazing sets and the craftsmanship was incredible. *Dumbo* was like nothing I'd ever seen. It was astonishing what they did. The Vandevere set was both interior and exterior, but all took place in this huge hangar in Cardington (England), which was used to build airships. The first time I walked onto it, they had prepared and choreographed a scene where myself and the kids arrive with Dumbo and the Medici Brothers Circus. It's this great big fair that Vandevere has created, so it's like Coney Island. There were 400 people lining up on the left and the right, 200 on either side, waving balloons. We came through these big gates in the back of a convertible, there were maybe 10 horses, four automobiles, a troupe of 60 to 80 dancing around us and we were walking down this boulevard of a theme park which was supposed to be outside in the real world. And it was all inside this hangar. It's kind of mind-bending.

What's Holt's relationship with Vandevere?

Vandevere is this all-powerful, successful, twisted Disney-like character who's world-famous and has this beautiful, extravagant theme park. He hears about this flying elephant and sees the potential to make a boatload of money. So he comes to Medici and offers to bring

07

> ## "Holt lost his left arm in battle, so he is both physically and psychologically wounded."

the whole troupe to his circus, to give them all jobs and put them all up – but it's a world that's overwhelming to the Medici troupe, and incredibly impersonal. It's totally run from the place of commercial enterprise and it's something that spoils pretty quick. Fairly early on, Vandevere cuts the rest of the troupe loose and just makes it a business about Dumbo. He also uses Holt's wounds against him. He uses his desire to be a horseman, and to re-experience some of the glories of his past. If Holt stands by Vandevere and does what's asked of him in relation to Dumbo, he'll make sure he gets a horse act again.

How was it playing someone missing an arm?

I basically just had a green sock on my left arm, and Richard (Stammers, visual effects supervisor) and his team of technological wizards removed it for the movie. It's something that initially Holt is hyper-aware of, and a little bit paranoid about. But as the story progresses, as he begins to accept the joy that his children are experiencing and the friendship that's growing between himself and Colette, Eva Green's character, the less this lack of a left arm seems to be an issue for him.

How was Eva Green to work with?

She's wonderful. She plays the part so beautifully. Colette and Holt are two different sides of the same coin. They both had to learn how to survive in a world that is harsh and judgmental and unforgiving. They both experienced moments of glory, and she is at the pinnacle of her success. But when we meet her in the film, her success is beginning to decline because Dumbo is coming in and taking the limelight.

How tough were the horse riding and roping scenes? Did they require significant training?

Any of the times I've ridden horses in films, there's always a specific reason or scene that will demand a certain new skill set. So I did a little bit of roping on this film that I hadn't really ever done before, and that was tricky. But I had some great guys working with me. Rowley (Irlam), who's the stunt coordinator, I worked with on *Alexander*, and Luis Miguel, who's a Spanish horse trainer and rider, is kind of a genius. So it was fun. It's a huge part of Holt's life, so it was fairly important that I at least seem to have a sense of comfort.

What do you hope audiences will get from watching this movie?

I hope people get a sense of buoyancy and a sense of seeing magic when they watch *Dumbo*, whatever age they may be. But a magic that's grounded in the reality of the interaction of all the human beings around this magical event that takes place. If that can wash over people, and if it can entertain them, then that's enough. 🐘

05 Tension in the Big Top: Holt faces off against Vandevere (Keaton) and his head of security, Skellig (Joseph Gatt).

06 Big-time showman V.A. Vandevere (Michael Keaton) shows Holt a possible bright new future.

07 Holt befriends Vandevere's aerialist star Colette Marchant (Eva Green).

THE AERIALIST

EVA GREEN

IS

COLETTE MARCHANT

The high-flying French star reveals the joys – and challenges – of swinging and spinning on a circus trapeze to play "The Queen of the Heavens."

02

01 Eva Green in full circus regalia as "Queen of the Heavens" Colette Marchant.

02 Green underwent intensive training to make her aerial work look "effortless."

Dumbo – The Official Movie Special: **Who do you play in** *Dumbo*?
Eva Green: I play Colette Marchant, a French aerialist. She's a huge star they call "The Queen of the Heavens" and she's also the girlfriend of Vandevere (Michael Keaton), who is the owner of Dreamland in Coney Island. When you first meet her she's quite mysterious, very star-like, quite haughty, quite superior. But beneath this cold exterior she reveals herself to be very brave and very kind.

Why does Colette connect with Holt (Colin Farrell) and the Farrier kids?
When Colette meets Holt for the first time she's quite dismissive, and she kind of looks down on him. She

doesn't believe Dumbo can fly. But when Vandevere puts her life at risk, she decides to join Holt's side and helps them save Dumbo and his mom.

Why do you think the original *Dumbo* **movie is still so beloved?**
I grew up with the animated version and I loved the story. The story between the baby elephant and the mother really marked me as a child. It's such a powerful, universal story, which both children and adults can connect with.

What was the most exciting thing about working on this film?
It is a Tim Burton movie! It's full of magic, full of poetry, and is very rich, moving, funny and spectacular.

How did you prepare for the role of Colette?
I had to train for four or five months to build a bit of muscle, because you have to be very strong as an aerialist. Your arms have to be quite strong, and you need strong abs as well. It's like dancing in the air. You try to find the right posture and the right gestures. I had the most amazing teachers: real circus people. That really helped me to get into the circus mood. Now I am an aerialist for real!

> "I was absolutely terrified of heights. It was a real phobia, and I told Tim at the beginning, 'I don't know if I will be able to do my stunts.'"

03 Colette forms a bond with Colin Farrell's Holt, sharing his concern for Dumbo.

04 She also grows close to Holt's children, including his son Joe (Finley Hobbins).

05

Was it hard to train as an aerialist?

I was absolutely terrified of heights. It was a real phobia, and I told Tim at the beginning, "I don't know if I will be able to do my stunts". But I trained with Catherine Arnold, who is the most amazing aerialist, and Fran James, who is the choreographer, and they really helped me to gain confidence and find the physicality of the character. It's unbelievable to swing up really high and spin and do some weird choreography. It was a real challenge and I'm quite proud of myself on that one.

Is it as difficult as it looks?

The challenge is to make it effortless, to look like it's so wonderful to be up there. But you really feel like the queen of the world in some way. You feel like a bird. There's something very freeing when you're up there. It's quite amazing.

Out of all the training you did, what was your favorite aspect?

My favorite bit of the training was doing the work in the air. Anything you do in the air becomes magical and graceful. I have to say that on this job all the training was very rewarding. It was such a physical role, and it was very jubilating, actually. I was never really a circus person before and now I'm addicted! I think I'm going to continue training as an aerialist in London. It's such a good workout as well.

05 Colette, in her black training ensemble, learns the secret of Dumbo's flying ability.

06 It's not easy at the top. Colette's status as the star of the show is initially threatened by Dumbo.

THE GREEN MILESTONES

THREE ESSENTIAL EVA GREEN PERFORMANCES

CASINO ROYALE (2006)

As Vesper Lynd, Eva Green was the ideal "Bond girl" for the first of Daniel Craig's 007 adventures, which modernized the spy series for the 21st Century. Initially resistant to his charms, and skeptical about his egotistical ways, Lynd might challenge Bond's methods, but she proves a valuable ally to the suave MI6 agent.

PENNY DREADFUL (2014)

As the psychic, troubled Vanessa Ives, Green was the lynchpin of this stylish, spooky gothic-horror mash-up TV show, always holding viewers' attention despite being surrounded by vampires, wolf men, and a Frankenstein's monster or two.

MISS PEREGRINE'S HOME FOR PECULIAR CHILDREN (2016)

For her second collaboration with Tim Burton (following 2012's *Dark Shadows*), Green played the quirky, crossbow-wielding headmistress who runs a home for kids with strange powers. Green's otherworldly style proved a perfect match for Burton's appealingly weird world.

What is Dreamland like?

It's a bit like Disney World. It's modern, it's big, it's brash, there's lots of money. And then you have the Medici Brothers Circus which is quite poor and tired, but it's got a heart. Dreamland was such an unbelievable set. What made it so wonderful was it was complete, which is quite rare these days, when sets are usually quite minimal. It was very real – you got all these attractions and all those amazing lights. It was a luxury to have real sets. You didn't have to imagine anything.

How was it working with real circus performers?

Every day I trained in the big tent and I could see contortionists warming up, clowns, the guy who throws knives… So I felt I was part of the circus. They worked so hard, I'm in total awe of them. I felt like I was going back to the golden era of Hollywood – there were hundreds of extras, clowns everywhere, dancers, horses. It was unbelievable.

What were the costumes like for you?

All my costumes are just so beautiful. I had these gold-and-red performance outfits, which made me feel like I was a ballerina on a jewelry box. So beautiful, very fairy-tale-like, with vibrant colors. It's very glamorous. (Costume designer) Colleen Atwood is a genius, and she did a magnificent job on this.

> "I felt like I was going back to the golden era of Hollywood — there were hundreds of extras, clowns everywhere, dancers, horses. It was unbelievable."

06

How did the costume design process with Colleen work?

On this job we had a few months, and Colleen was very open. She wants the actors to feel comfortable. I emailed her a few ideas and, of course, she added her magic. What's interesting about Colette is she has these amazing, glamorous, theatrical outfits, with dramatic red wigs. But underneath she has this simple black bob. When she trains, she's just in a black leotard. It's very simple. So it was really interesting to have those different facets to the character.

How does Colette's relationship with Dumbo evolve?

When Colette sees Dumbo for the first time she's quite skeptical. She thinks his flying is a trick, but when she discovers he really can fly she changes her attitude completely and grows to love him.

What was it like working with Danny DeVito, who plays Medici?

He's such a joy to work with. I had to pinch myself all the time. He's so free. He's always having fun. He's such an inspiration. I wished he could be on set every day, because there's so much positive energy exuding from him.

How about Michael Keaton?

Mr. Michael Keaton is bonkers in a lovely way. He's so charismatic and irreverent. Again, I had to pinch myself – I was thinking, "Oh my god, he's Beetlejuice. Wow!" These are iconic actors. It was hard for me to stay in character!

What message does this movie send to people about embracing others' differences?

(Whistles) Ooh la la! Dumbo is a very Tim Burton movie – it encourages you to embrace your uniqueness, your individuality. You don't need to be perfect to be loved. And it also tells kids to believe in themselves. If you believe in yourself, you can overcome any obstacle. It's very Disney! (Laughs)

Why do you think Dumbo is such great material for a filmmaker like Tim Burton?

He's an iconic director, a poet, who always brings a unique vision, and he's perfect for this movie because nobody better understands people who don't fit in. He understands vulnerable souls like Dumbo.

How exactly is Tim Burton's vision for this movie unique?

I loved the original version, but Tim's new version is a different take on it, and Tim always brings lots of surprises, magic, humor, and emotion. It remains very moving. This is such a powerful story, and I think the baby elephant will melt everyone's hearts. ⊞

MICHAEL KEATON

IS

V.A. VANDEVERE

After making three movies with Tim Burton during the '80s and '90s, Michael Keaton is back for a fourth team-up as *Dumbo*'s sinister showman V.A. Vandevere. But, in the case of this film, being the bad guy didn't come easy to him…

02

03

04

Dumbo – The Official Movie Special: **What initially drew you to this project?**
Michael Keaton: Two words. Or two names, I guess: Tim and Burton (*laughs*). We worked together three times before. This is the fourth. He's not only a friend, I also think the experience of working with someone like Tim – although there actually is no one like Tim – is something most actors would jump at. It's always a really good experience for me to be around that kind of creativity, vision, and imagination. When you're working on a set with Tim, and the people he hires to surround him, you're reminded of why you do what you do.

What about the attraction of *Dumbo* itself?
The classic story I'm somewhat familiar with, but I'm not a *Dumbo* aficionado. In fact, I'm kind of a "dumbo" when it comes to that. But this is a really sweet story and the script was really emotional and well written.

This movie reunites you with Tim and Danny DeVito for the first time since 1992's *Batman Returns*. Did you discuss that?

> "The irony is, I love elephants. I thought, 'I can't do this. I can't be that bad guy.'"

There was no discussion: "Hey, this is what we're going to do." I wasn't part of it anyway, if there was one (*laughs*). It was just, "Hey, Tim Burton's making a movie," so I paid attention to that. Frankly, I didn't think I would be able to do this, because I was finishing something else, and there was something I was preparing for in the future. But your ears always perk up a little bit when Tim's name is mentioned and you think, "Well, maybe I'll just take a look at the script…" And then when I'd read the script, I thought, "Well, I better figure out a way to make this work." There are certain people, when they call, you really want it to work if you can. There have been opportunities with other great directors where I just couldn't do it, which was disappointing to say the least. But we slid this into a window and I'm glad. It's just fun to show up for work and be part of all of this.

What was it like being part of this particular Tim Burton movie?
This film is huge. I didn't know what was going on behind the scenes, because there was a lot to put together, but it all just seemed to fall into place every day. The ▶

THE KEATON-BURTON CHEMISTRY

BEFORE *DUMBO*, THE DIRECTOR AND STAR TEAMED UP FOR THESE THREE CLASSICS…

BEETLEJUICE (1988)

Burton's second-ever movie is a gothic horror-comedy, which stars Keaton as an obnoxious, clownish specter hired by a kindly ghost couple (Alec Baldwin and Geena Davis) to help scare off the ghastly (in a different sense) family who moved into their house. In Halloween makeup, with a wild spray of green hair, Keaton is barely recognizable, but is the (after)life of the party throughout.

BATMAN (1989)

Beetlejuice's success made Burton the surprise choice to direct super hero blockbuster *Batman*. And Keaton was his even-more-surprising choice to play the title character, given he was previously best known for comedies.

People complained he wasn't right for the costumed vigilante, but Keaton proved them wrong, not only portraying a convincingly brooding and menacing Batman, but also holding his own against Jack Nicholson's larger-than-life Joker.

BATMAN RETURNS (1992)

Keaton and Burton reunited for the sequel, which brought in Danny DeVito (another Burton regular who also stars in *Dumbo*) as the villainous Penguin and Michelle Pfeiffer as an unforgettable Catwoman. Once again, Keaton proved he could match his villain-playing co-stars blow for blow. It was the last time either the star or director would make a *Batman*, but they sure went out with a bang.

01 Michael Keaton's character, circus impresario V.A. Vandevere, has plenty to reflect on in the new *Dumbo* movie…

02 Keaton as Vandevere, reading about a certain miraculous elephant.

03 Vandevere with his pre-Dumbo star attraction, trapeze artist Colette Marchant (Eva Green).

04 Vandevere convinces Max Medici to sell up.

05

05 Vandevere with the Farrier kids (Nico Parker and Finley Hobbins) and his right-hand man Skellig (Joseph Gatt).

06 Vandevere looks on as his big show goes up in flames.

07 The Farriers and Max Medici (Danny DeVito) make their entrance into Dreamland.

craftsmanship of the artistry involved was unbelievable – particularly of Colleen Atwood (the costume designer), who is incredible. One day I walked onto one of the sets with, if I'm not mistaken, 1,500 extras, and I looked at everyone's wardrobe and it was just so specific and wonderful, right down to heels on shoes. It's the same for every department. It's really a pleasure to be around these kinds of people. And that comes from Tim Burton. People want to be in that world and he has a good sense of who to hire and why it's great.

How did Tim describe the movie to you when you first talked about it?
He told me that it's about family. That is the theme, really. One reason Vandevere, my character, behaves the way he behaves – which is not too nice – is he never really had a family, and deep inside that ate him up.

Although, he would never let you know that. And there's this little circus family that's not a "mom, dad, and two kids" situation. The father, played by Colin Farrell, is trying to hold this little family together. Enter this really cute little flying elephant. You've got forces who want to grow that and enjoy that and make that a wonderful thing. Then there are some people who want to exploit it for their own personal profit (*laughs*). Unfortunately, I'm that guy...

Was it hard to play someone who's so willing to exploit such a sweet creature as Dumbo?
The irony is, I love elephants. I thought, "I can't do this. I can't be that bad guy." I don't know if you've ever seen an elephant in the wild, in their natural habitat. It's mind-blowing. They'll stop you right in your tracks. They're great! 🐘

06

"It's always a good experience for me to be around
Tim Burton's creativity, vision, and imagination."

07

THE RINGMASTER

DANNY DEVITO

AS

MAX MEDICI

Veteran star Danny DeVito makes the Big Top feel bigger than it's ever been before as the circus showman who discovers a certain flying elephant. Here he shares the joys of living in Tim Burton's worlds and his abiding love for the original movie.

02

03

Dumbo – The Official Movie Special: Who do you play in *Dumbo*?

Danny DeVito: I play Max Medici, the owner of Medici Brothers Circus. It's a little circus that travels all around the country in the Southern United States. It has elephants, a couple of dogs, a snake, some really great contortionists and high-wire acts, and all kinds of cool jugglers and clowns. But it's right after the First World War and it's very difficult to make ends meet in the circus, so people are pitching in and doing other jobs to help out, because they are a family and they're trying to make the circus work. The strongman is Max's accountant! Then Max makes an investment and Mrs. Jumbo comes to the circus and thank goodness she's pregnant. And she gives birth to you-know-who.

Tell us about the journey Medici goes on in this film.

In the very beginning, the Medici Brothers Circus is very worn, like a shirt that you've had forever that you love and you never want to throw away. And then it's swallowed up by Vandevere's circus. He comes in and takes them out of the doldrums. There are some very suspicious machinations to this – it's not quite what they think. They probably should have just stuck to their guns, but Max figures he'll make a few bucks. Then they go to the big, glitzy circus with all the money and all the big investors. They take the Medici Brothers Circus over and, of course, the big attraction is Dumbo – I mean, everybody wants a piece of Dumbo. That's all there is to it.

This isn't the first time you've played a circus ringmaster for Tim Burton, is it?

Well, this is our circus trilogy, Tim and I. I had a circus troupe in *Batman Returns*. Then we did *Big Fish* along the way, and I was the circus ringmaster in that. Now this is a completion of the circle. Not to say we won't do other circuses together, but this feels like we're making it whole!

How was it working with Michael Keaton on this movie?

It was cool. This is my third movie with Michael. We did *Johnny Dangerously*, we did *Batman Returns*, and this. In *Batman Returns*, Keaton was Batman and I was The Penguin. A lot of people thought I was the bad guy; I didn't think I was the bad guy as The Penguin, but they did. So now it's reversed, because I'm playing the good guy for sure in this movie, and Michael Keaton is the bad guy. We had a lot of fun.

How was it working with the other cast: Colin Farrell, Eva Green, and the kids?

Colin Farrell's terrific to work with. I've known him for many years, but we've never actually worked together before. *Dumbo* has a great cast of people. It was a lot of fun to be in there with Eva Green, and the kids were great. They were so funny, these kids. They came up with all these little games to play, you know?

How was it to work on such a visual effects-intensive movie?

This was a totally different thing for me. I've never done anything that combines live action with CG – all our elephants are made in the ones-and-zeros world. It was very interesting to see the way it's done. For instance, you'd be in a scene and Dumbo had to be right here. You couldn't invade that space as an actor. They had these big, green aluminum frames that were covered with green fabric which represented the elephants, and somebody wearing a green suit would walk them around, and you had to stay beyond the perimeter of those things. It was really cool.

Did you have an idea of what Dumbo looked like in this film?

I'd seen models of Dumbo – they made models so you could see what you were looking at. They had a Mrs. Jumbo, too. They have shops at Pinewood Studios (in England) that they build all this stuff in. I also saw the pre-viz, which is the animated line drawings, basically, of the scenes with the elephant flying, so you got a feeling of what it's like to see that in the tent.

What was it like working on the sets designed by Tim and production designer Rick Heinrichs?

The sets were magnificent! There are always layers in Tim's movies, like dualities, not only in the characters but ▶

01 Danny DeVito as Max Medici: a great showman in style, if not stature.

02 Max, with Farrier father Holt (Colin Farrell) and daughter Milly (Nico Parker) watching Dumbo fly.

03 Danny DeVito as the ringmaster of the Medici Brothers Circus.

04 Max shows off an elephant-sized rattle for our baby-elephant hero.

05

THE BURTON–DEVITO CONNECTION

DUMBO IS NOT THE FIRST TIME DANNY DEVITO HAS WORKED WITH TIM BURTON...

BATMAN RETURNS (1992)
DeVito all but disappeared beneath elaborate prosthetics to play Oswald Cobblepot: a grotesque and psychopathic villain better known as The Penguin, in the darkest of all the early _Batman_ movies. DeVito was suggested for the role by his friend Jack Nicholson, who played the Joker in Burton's first _Batman_.

MARS ATTACKS! (1996)
DeVito appears in Burton's crazy and audacious ensemble sci-fi comedy as "Rude Gambler," rubbing shoulders with Annette Bening, Jim Brown, and Welsh crooner Tom Jones. As it was such a huge cast (with Jack Nicholson appearing in two different roles), this was DeVito's smallest role for Burton – though he was memorably disintegrated by a Martian ray gun.

BIG FISH (2003)
In Burton's beautiful and affecting story of a man trying to untangle the real events of his traveling-salesman father's life from his many tall tales, DeVito appears as a circus ringmaster named Amos Calloway. He's a rather different ringmaster from the one he plays in _Dumbo_, however, especially when he's revealed as being a werewolf.

06

07

in the texture of the sets, too. You've got the dark, really rich stuff, and then there's that whimsical part of Tim that comes out that is really cool. Interestingly, there's a "D" on everything. There were things with "Ds" on them everywhere I looked. Disney, DeVito, Dumbo!

How about the costumes?
The costumes are amazing, thanks to Colleen Atwood, the brilliant costumer. I had ten great costumes that were just amazing. There's a feeling of progression, where it goes from that pair of shoes that you wore forever, and you give them up for something better. So the costumes change, and do you really change with them or are they just added on? Colleen's costumes reflect the personality of the whole troupe. My daughter Lucy is in the movie playing a hat-check girl and her costume is so cute and beautiful, but very detailed.

What was it like working with the performers who make up Medici's troupe?
They are the most talented jugglers and tumblers and acrobats and high-wire artists I've ever seen. It was so great to be around them. They were constantly doing cartwheels and flips, and guys were balancing chairs and walking like cats on stuff. It's amazing when people have such control over their body that they can do all that stuff. But me, I'm happy just sitting in this chair.

What do you think of the original, animated *Dumbo* movie?
I watched it when I was a kid, and I've got three kids, so I've watched it many times over the years. And I watched it again after Tim called me about playing Medici. It always gives you a tear in your eye, with Mrs. Jumbo and when Dumbo's born. She's so left out at the beginning, the stork is not bringing her babies. She's so sad and then finally Dumbo comes and of course he comes with an added attraction: he's got these big, blanket ears that just go on forever but, you know, it's unrequited love. That's what we have for our kids and that's what this movie is all about. There is such artistry in that movie, and if anybody can remake it, Tim can. It's going to be off the charts, really spectacular. 𝕯

> "There are always layers in Tim's movies. You've got the dark, really rich stuff, and then there's that whimsical part of Tim that comes out that is really cool."

05 Circus owner Max Medici (Danny DeVito) in full-on "huckster" mode. What he lacks in style, he makes up for with enthusiasm!

06 Medici and his elephant caretaker Holt don't always agree.

07 A troubled Max watches Dumbo in action, with financier J. Griffin Remington (Alan Arkin) and Vandevere (Michael Keaton).

This dramatic piece of concept art reveals the fiery consequences of V.A. Vandevere's (Michael Keaton) exploitation of Dumbo. As his empire burns, the heroic little elephant flies free.

NICO PARKER

★ AND ★

FINLEY HOBBINS

ARE

MILLY AND JOE

Dumbo's youngest stars reveal what it was like to enter the fantastical world of the Big Top – and why they won't be running away with a real circus any time soon.

02

03

Dumbo – The Official Movie Special: **How was this film's audition process for you both?**
Nico Parker: I did about four auditions. The first was a self-tape, which I preferred, because I wasn't nervous. I wasn't meeting anyone, so I was fine. And then I got a callback, which is when I first met Tim Burton, and that was terrifying! Then I did three more auditions, where I met Fin, who plays my younger brother. And from there it all went really quickly.
Finley Hobbins: For my first audition I had to perform a scene with a fake Dumbo, which was actually (casting director) Susie Figgis' dog, 'cos we didn't actually have a model of Dumbo. Every few seconds the dog would jiggle around and we'd have a laugh. I had to do the scene where Dumbo is just sitting around, feeling quite sad and lonely, so Nico and I go to comfort him.

What was it like when you heard you'd got the part?
Parker: I'd just got home from school one day and they said, "You got the part!" And I thought, "Whoa, this is so cool!" It's an honor to have this as my first film. It's such a huge production and an incredible movie.
Hobbins: I was lying in bed in the morning and my mum came to wake me up. She said, "Guess what, Fin? You got the part!" But I didn't believe her. Then she actually showed me the email and I said, "Oh my God."

Who do you both play in this movie?
Hobbins: I play Joe and he's a bit of a crazy, clumsy little boy. He's quite energetic and exciting, which I like.
Parker: I play Milly, who is very driven and hard working. She loves science, which is a cool thing, and she feels like she's in the wrong shoes, or the wrong place. She actually doesn't have any interest in all the circus acts, despite growing up in the circus.

What is life like for Milly and Joe when we first meet them in the story?
Parker: When it first starts, their mom has recently passed away, and Milly and her brother, although they have an incredible support system of everyone at the circus around them, are technically left alone.
Hobbins: Their dad (Colin Farrell) wasn't there when their mom died, because he was at war, so it's been quite hard for Joe and Milly. Then when their dad comes back, they are really excited. They run to him, but when they see him they suddenly stop, because they see he only has one arm. They're a bit freaked out, but they learn to get along with him.

What was it like working with Colin Farrell, who plays your father Holt?
Parker: What I liked about working with Colin was how insanely nice he was all the time. He's such an incredibly

great star, but he's so down to earth, and so understanding. For example, if I got a line wrong, he was just very kind to me about it.

What have you enjoyed most about being part of the Medici Brothers Circus in this movie?

Parker: The Medici Brothers Circus was amazing. There were some incredibly talented people: contortionists and knife throwers and jugglers – people who had balls on their heads and just danced around. There was such a vast palette of talents throughout the whole circus, and it really was incredible to see how they did everything.

Hobbins: I liked the clowns, who were quite freaky and funny, and the contortionists, who were amazing. I just thought to myself: "Wow, what if *I* could do that?"

Why is Dumbo such an outsider when he first arrives at the circus?

Hobbins: Everyone gives him a hard time, like, "Ah, this is useless. We can't use him in our show because of his ears," so that makes him quite sad. But also his mom's taken away, which means he's having a very hard time.

Parker: At first people don't really know how to deal with Dumbo's exceptionally large ears. They just think it's weird and don't really want him. But then he learns to fly and that is an incredible gift.

Why do you think Milly and Joe care for Dumbo so much?

Hobbins: They've been through a similar experience: their mother died when they were little, and his mother was taken away. So they know how it feels and don't want Dumbo to go through what they've been through.

Parker: Milly and Joe show him that they're always there for him, even at the times when he doesn't believe in himself. They're so immensely proud of him that when he isn't proud of himself, they make sure he knows he's incredible. Also, they know what it's like to lose a mother, so they constantly sympathize with what he's going through.

> "It's an honor to have this as my first film. It's such a huge production and an incredible movie."
>
> *Nico Parker*

What was it like working with Dumbo on set?

Hobbins: At first, I thought there would be an elephant and I was thinking, "Yeah, woohoo!" But then I realized that it's a man called Edd, who was in a green suit which would be turned into an elephant on-screen.

Parker: Edd was really nice. He acted like an elephant most of the time. I don't know how he did it. He was very intricate, and when he ran it honestly looked like he was about to take off!

How is Vandevere's Dreamland different from the Medici Brothers Circus? ▶

01 Joe (Finley Hobbins) and Milly (Nico Parker) take a peek behind the curtain.

02 When their father Holt (Colin Farrell) returns from the First World War, it's quite an awkward family reunion.

03 The Farrier kids are understandably impressed when they first lay eyes on Vandevere's (Michael Keaton) Dreamland.

Parker: It is huge compared to the Medici Brothers Circus and is fancier. Everything there is more expensive and bigger and better.

Hobbins: Dreamland is a *lot* bigger. There are many more acts and there's more color and excitement, with all these great adverts and posters and people.

What was it like working with Tim Burton on this movie?

Hobbins: Tim is definitely a fun character to work with, because he's always very exciting and creative and full of ideas – always jumping around the place. It's nice to have someone directing you who's so joyful.

Parker: At first, I was so intimidated because he is such a big director. I thought, "This is Tim Burton. I've watched all his movies!" (*Laughs*) But he was so nice.

How have you both gotten along together, working with each other?

Hobbins: Nico's definitely a character. On or off set, we were messing around. We always had a lot of fun together. We were never bored. We had a few jokes, though we did tease each other a lot, too. I felt like we had a brother-sister relationship.

Parker: I spent so much time with Fin that after a while he really did seem like my little brother. I felt like I could tell him anything, and he was always there to talk to me. Also, he was one of the only other kids on set, which was cool, because if he hadn't been there I would have just been surrounded by grown-ups. I really liked working with Fin.

Have either of you ever been to a real circus? Did you enjoy the experience?

Hobbins: I've been to Gifford's Circus, which was very cool. There were all these people doing backflips from swings onto people's shoulders. Also, the thing about circuses is not only do they do incredible things, but they also act while they're doing it. They add a bit of personality to the show.

Parker: I've been to a couple and I think they're incredible. The performers are so talented and I think, "How are you doing that?"

Do you have any circus talents? Would you run away and join the circus?

Parker: I do dance, and I've been doing it for a while now. But I don't think I'm quite good enough to run off and join a circus.

Hobbins: I wish. I'd be totally busted if I did that. I've had to learn how to juggle, which in the movie I am terrible at – and that's a good thing, because I am also terrible at juggling in real life.

Did you have any stunts you needed to do as part of this film?

Parker: I did one really cool stunt where I climbed up a ladder and there's fire, and there's water. It was a 32-foot ladder which seems really scary, but I thought it was really fun. People said, "Oh, be really careful!" and I just replied, "No, I've got this. Don't worry. I'll be fine." I had a wire on while I was going up, just in case.

04

05

What were your impressions of all the sets on this production?

Parker: The sets were so incredible. The attention to detail about every single thing was crazy. I remember going on to the Vandevere's circus set and thinking, "This is a *big* movie." Everything was just so big and I don't know how they did it. I'd never seen anything like it.

Hobbins: The sets were definitely one of the best parts of making the film. They were enormous. It was never not exciting at all, it was never just all right. It was always mind-blowing, what they did. Dreamland's got to be my favorite. There was so much to do in Dreamland, and there was fake food – which tasted good, by the way.

What were the costumes like?

Hobbins: The costumes in this movie are brilliant. They are like they were made a hundred years ago. Every time I got a new costume, I thought, "Yes!" I was either always wearing baggy trousers and braces, or dungarees. One of my favorite costumes was a red suit which came with a cowboy hat, and I was like a real cowboy.

Parker: Colette (Eva Green)'s costumes are incredible. I want all of them. They're really amazing and the amount of time and effort that went into all of it is really incredible.

Have you seen the original *Dumbo*?

Hobbins: I have. I did like it, but I was quite confused

> "Tim Burton is definitely a fun character to work with. He's always very exciting and creative and full of ideas."
> *Finley Hobbins*

because I watched it when I was a little kid. Then I watched it again before the movie, just to get a little recap of what it was about.

Parker: I am a fan of the original *Dumbo*, but I really do think of this as a completely different story, because they've really changed it.

Why should we be excited about this movie?

Hobbins: First of all you should be excited because all the Tim Burton movies I've seen have been incredible. Also, *Dumbo* is a really big adventure. If you've seen the cartoon, you know it's a big adventure.

Parker: I think probably the coolest thing about this film would be how incredible the cast are, and the production is, and how when you put it all together it creates this really amazing thing that I'm so honored to be part of. That's what I would probably tell my friends. If they ask, "Why should I watch this movie?" I'll say, "*That's* why." (*Laughs*) 🄳

04 Milly (Parker) goes to great lengths – or rather, heights – to help Dumbo.

05 The Farrier family, in the heat of a dangerous moment.

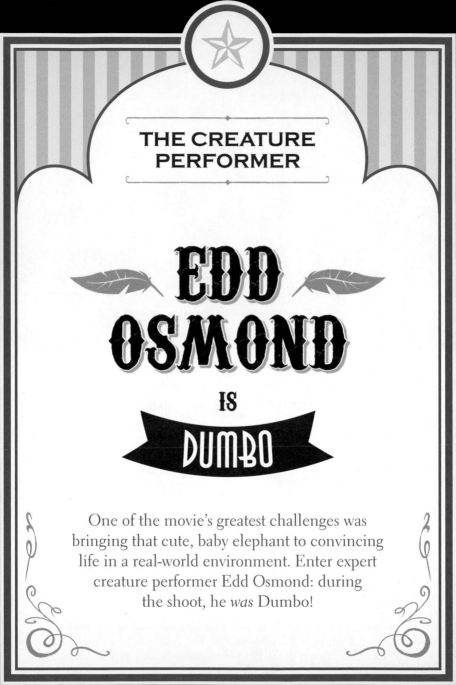

THE CREATURE PERFORMER

EDD OSMOND

IS

DUMBO

One of the movie's greatest challenges was bringing that cute, baby elephant to convincing life in a real-world environment. Enter expert creature performer Edd Osmond: during the shoot, he *was* Dumbo!

Dumbo – The Official Movie Special: **How would you sum up your role on this production?**
Edd Osmond: My job was probably the strangest job of everyone on the film. I played Dumbo on set – I was responsible for all his movements and I provided the eyeline for the other actors. Because Dumbo's obviously a CG (computer-generated) character, a lot of my movements were transferred onto Dumbo himself.

What precisely did that involve for you?
We had seven or eight different versions of the character, and for each version we had two different sizes, because Dumbo starts off as a really small elephant and then, midway through, he grows up into a bigger-sized elephant. One of the costumes I had to wear was a padded performance suit with a big elephant head, which represents a real, life-size Dumbo. The only problem was, once I was in the suit I had to look down while I was on all fours, which meant I had no vision at all. So the special makeup and effects guys came up with these special goggles for me, which were linked up to a little video camera in the top of the elephant, which meant I could always see a live feed of what was going

on. I had a utility belt as well, and inside there was a little mic pouch which went to the VFX guys, who constantly spoke to me. If I was going to knock Colin [Farrell] over, they'd say, "Stop, stop, stop," in my ear. That's just one version of the costume, which we had in gray, blue and green Lycra.

Can you give us some examples of the other suits you had to wear?
Originally, we had me in gray tracksuit bottoms and a gray hoodie with gray arm extensions and we thought, "That'll give the VFX guys enough to work off." Then we stepped up a gear, with a green Lycra suit with this massive head and really big ears, like a wire version of Dumbo. We also had a waterproof version, which we called "Stealth Dumbo" because it's black. That was for when I had to do the bath scene.

What's your background?
I've done a lot of creature work before. I've done different animals, I've done goblins. I've been in a lot of heavy prosthetic makeup, which is what I normally do. Every time you do a job and think, "This is as weird as it gets," you get a call about a month later and it gets weirder.

What happened when you got the call for this?
I got the call on my birthday, and I was told I was coming in for a meeting about "Big Ears." I had no idea what it was. I had an idea that it was going to be this big goblin creature or something. I walked into the workshop and in the distance I saw elephant heads absolutely everywhere. I thought, "Okay, okay, I think it's *Dumbo*." Then after I spoke for about half an hour with David White, who ▶

01 Dumbo was brought to life on the film set by Edd Osmond.

02 Osmond in his green Dumbo costume, alongside Tim Burton and a life-size reference model of Dumbo. (Photo: Jay Maidment)

03 Osmond in action in his performance suit, as the angry crowd throw things at Dumbo. (Photo: Jay Maidment)

04 Dumbo initially enjoys his circus life, as depicted in this concept painting.

05 Dumbo's special circus sign, missing a letter.

06

06 Concept art
showing Dumbo
with Mrs. Jumbo.

07 Dumbo swoops
over the astonished
circus crowd in this
concept painting.

heads up our special makeup and effects, we turned a corner and there was this life-sized cast of Dumbo. Two seconds later, I'm standing in this cast of an elephant, and from that moment I was Dumbo!

What's the trick to doing good creature work?

The key is just letting yourself completely go. You have to be adaptable, because anything you think you're prepared for, you never are. It will always change. When you do creature movement, usually you'll do a couple of weeks of rehearsals prior to filming to get that movement down.

So when you're on set and the director asks you to run in a certain direction, you can pick up straight away.

What are the challenges of portraying an elephant, specifically?

Elephants are on all fours and they have a lot of weight on their front shoulders, which means when you're doing long, 12-hour days, it can be very tiring on the shoulders. So at the end of the day, there's a lot of baths and a lot of Epsom salts.

How much did you refer to the original film as part of your research?

I hadn't seen the original film for about 15 years, so I watched it and I think I got a little bit too emotionally invested in the character. When you watch the cartoon, Dumbo is really light and fairy-like. He's always got a little lift to his steps. The next day I came in and I said, "Guys, I've done some research. I know how Dumbo walks." So, stupidly, I gathered an audience, and I put on the elephant head and costume, and I started running around with my new lift that I had created overnight, practicing in the mirror. When I came out of the costume, they said, "We won't do that, because it just doesn't look real." It was then that I realized that you have to keep your performance true to the original, but you also have to make it feel real, especially for the actors on set so they know what they're dealing with. That's probably one of the biggest challenges.

How much did you study the movement of real elephants in your research?

I did a lot of elephant research. I watched a lot of videos, and looked at babies in particular, because Dumbo is a baby elephant. Where an adult elephant is definite in the way its feet are going, if you watch baby elephants, a lot of the time they're stumbling, they're going back and forward. Which is actually one thing I had to work on, because when you put on arm extensions and you have all your weight on them, trying to stumble and make it look convincing and not actually break your arm is a real struggle. I think I spent a week practicing in a little office room, just walking like a drunk elephant!

What other challenges did you encounter while playing Dumbo?

I had to learn not to keep moving, because a moving elephant is so distracting from the scene, and a lot of the time I just had to stand still, knowing visual effects would animate the trunk or the eyes so he's interacting with the characters. Another hard thing that I didn't

> "You have to keep your performance true to the original movie, but you also have to make it feel real."

anticipate was the trunk. Having a trunk caused so many problems. If I was about three feet away from the camera, I felt like that was a good space, but what I wasn't thinking of was Dumbo's trunk. So sometimes when I was in the performance suit, I'd do a quick startle turn to the right to look at Colin and I'd feel an odd thud, and realize I'd hit a camera with the trunk. So spatial awareness was a huge thing.

Given Dumbo can fly as well as just walk, what were all the different kinds of movements you had to do while playing him?

We had so many different types of movement for Dumbo: pre-flight mode, post-flight mode, walking, running, stumbling. We even had a bath mode, for when Dumbo was being bathed, which was a whole different world in itself. Probably the hardest mode was post-flight. I had to mimic that instant jolt down to the floor, and if you're going at fast speed you have to continue that speed and slow down. So if I was on a smaller set and Dumbo entered the scene from flight mode, I had to keep that pace up, but then also try and stop in time before I hit the camera.

How was Dumbo's mother, Mrs. Jumbo, realized on set?

David White came up with this amazing, life-sized Mrs. Jumbo performance suit. It looked great. I've no idea how they made this work, but inside Mrs. Jumbo there were two people: someone up front moving the front legs, and someone at the back moving the back legs. And I thought *my* job was hard!

How difficult did you find it connecting with the other actors while being on all fours in the Dumbo costume?

It was very difficult to portray an elephant on set and hear what was going on around me, or get eye contact with the actors. But as far as physical interaction goes, it was quite easy to do, because all of the cast were so lovely with Dumbo and they were very hands on. If I couldn't see them, they were touching me or guiding me, which was great, because that's what the character is like: he's very young and he doesn't know his way. So I think sometimes me not being able to see perfectly kind of added to the character.

What do you miss most about portraying the character of Dumbo?

I miss the character so much. Because Dumbo is so young, I had so much freedom to do whatever I felt like at the time, during the scenes. People would say, "Well, he's young. He doesn't know where he's going." It was really nice to have complete freedom with a character – and to know that if I did anything wrong, they'd fix it in post! (*Laughs*)

THE EVIL SIDEKICK

JOSEPH GATT

IS

★ NEILS SKELLIG ★

The British character actor reveals how he
got bad to the bone to play V.A. Vandevere's
animal-hating right-hand man.

02

Dumbo – The Official Movie Special: How familiar are you with the original, animated *Dumbo* movie?

Joseph Gatt: I only watched it for the first time about three weeks before flying out to London for filming – which is strange, because I'm a huge Disney lover. I'm also a massive animal lover, especially elephants! (*Laughs*) Obviously, it's a great movie, but very much of its time. I think Ehren Kruger did an amazing job with our script because he's taken all of the cute, loveable, memorable aspects of the original and modernized it. Even though it's set in the same time period, it feels modern in the messages it's delivering, with regards to how we feel about animals, people, and family today, as opposed to how we felt about those things 70 years ago.

Who do you play in the film?

I play Neils Skellig, who is basically Darth Vader to V.A. Vandevere (Michael Keaton)'s Emperor. He is a pretty horrible person. He doesn't like animals very much, unlike myself, so it made it a very interesting acting challenge for me. He's based on the stereotypical great white South African hunter. Skellig has a South African accent, and it's the first time I've done that accent on

camera. It's been a lot of fun. But I'm concerned that I'm not going to be able to go to a Disney park after this movie is released – I'm going to be hated by everyone! (*Laughs*)

What makes Skellig so bad?

He is Vandevere's head of security and also supervises the procurement of the animals and attractions for Vandevere's Dreamland. But it's not always a pleasant job...

Did you worry about making him *too* bad?

For my audition, my agent told me what Tim Burton wanted to see from Skellig, which was "this horrible, nasty character." I said, "Okay, but do you want me to pull it back a little bit, because it's Disney?" She replied, "No. They want you to go for it." So I went for it and they loved it. Apparently, Tim saw the tape and said, "That's the guy. He hates animals. That's the actor for Skellig!"

What was it like working with Tim Burton?

It's been an incredible experience. A dream acting job. He's like a dad. He's so in charge, and yet one of the most comfortable directors I've ever worked with. His movies are all incredible, and you always appreciate his artistry. All his films have a very particular style about them. I had

"Skellig is basically Darth Vader to V.A. Vandevere's Emperor. He is a pretty horrible person."

a lot of questions for Tim, because it would be all too easy to play Skellig as the melodramatic, over-the-top bad guy, and that's neither my personal style nor would have been my preference for this character.

I was really pleased when I met Tim, and one of the first things he said to me was, "You're going to be frightening enough just by doing nothing – just by being." I said, "Oh. I think that's a compliment. That's perfect!" (*Laughs*)

How do your character and Holt (Colin Farrell) regard each other in the film?

It's a strange relationship between Skellig and Holt. At first he respects Holt. He served. He lost an arm. But after a while Holt gets on Skellig's nerves. He's getting in the way of this so-called magical creature, and Skellig has to keep reminding Holt that he doesn't give the orders here. He's in Skellig's house now.

How did you find doing the South African accent?

Changing my voice and my accent is almost normal for me now. I was born and raised in London, but since moving to Los Angeles 15 years ago I've only once played a role on camera with a British accent,

and that was for *Game of Thrones*. I play Americans a lot – including various regional accents like Cajun and American Southern – but have also played a lot of Germans, Russians, and now a South African. I was already familiar with the South African accent, because I have some family members who grew up there. We also had a voice coach, Roisin (Carty) on set, and she's incredible. I was originally working with a very strong South African accent, but Tim decided that something more subtle would be a better fit for the character, so Roisin and I worked on dialing back the accent while still keeping it distinct and present. I was very happy with the end result.

03

How would you describe the cast as a whole?

One word springs to mind: perfect. I cannot think of a more perfect casting for any of the roles. It was "Dreamland." Working on a show like this with Tim, the cast, the crew, the sets, the costumes, etc., and all at Pinewood... It's a dream job. I could not imagine a better job, unless they gave me a horse to ride in every shot. That would be great. Or a Ferrari. Skellig should have had a Ferrari he went hunting in! (*Laughs*)

What should we most be looking forward to about seeing this film?

Well, if this film is going to be 90 minutes long, you're going to look forward to 90 minutes of laughing, crying, and a few other emotions in between, and then you're going to leave the cinema with a very happy and warm feeling. Everyone's going to hate Skellig, and they're going to hate Vandevere, but it's going to be a lovely movie. There are worse things in life than being a Disney Villain! 🅳

MAKING AN ELEPHANT FLY

BEHIND THE SCENES:

TIM BURTON'S VISION

Shot entirely on the soundstages of Pinewood and Cardington Studios in England, *Dumbo* represents a colossal artistic and technical achievement which required the careful coordination of every filmmaking department.

In the following pages, we go behind the red curtain to reveal how they brought this Disney animated classic into the live-action world, from the scriptwriting, to the production design, to the costume design, to the visual effects.

★ RICK ★
HEINRICHS

From the warmth of the Medici Brothers Circus to the cold futurism of Vandevere's Dreamland, the world of *Dumbo* is one of spectacular contrasts. Tim Burton's long-time production designer Rick Heinrichs reveals how they conjured it all up.

Rick Heinrichs: "*Dumbo* is a favorite film of mine from the Disney vaults. It deals with its story and characters in such a delightfully emotional and beautifully graphic way that I was excited to figure out how we could bring a new version of it to life. Tim's stylistic tendency is toward expressionism and that's been a big factor in this film. We were inspired to some degree by the original animated film, but a big part of our task here was to create a believable live-action world which a flying elephant could reasonably inhabit.

"At the emotional core of the film was the basic contrast and conflict of character and environment represented by the Medici Brothers Circus and Vandevere's destination park Dreamland – requiring a visual divergence akin almost to Dorothy's Kansas and the Land of Oz.

"The Medici Brothers Circus troupe is a family, so there's a warmth we wanted to convey, both through color and in the ways the scenes were shot. It's not all happy warmth, though – there's definitely contrast and shadow that the troupe and the Farrier family endure. We wanted there to be a palpable tug between the inherent joy and wonder of promised pleasures that a circus represents and the sobering realities inflicted upon the circus and its family by the circumstances of the sad, harsh period. The Medici Big Top itself is designed to feel a little hard on its luck, that there's something a bit slumped over and wistful about it, but at the same time it's still certainly trying to put on a good show for the local audience.

"In stark repudiation of that is the optimistic futurism of Dreamland. Its exotic attractions are truly wondrous to behold, but are ultimately undercut by a manipulative and greedy emotional core that is embodied by its impresario and his associates. There is a bright, colder palette and harder, reflective texture to Vandevere's world, one that is as spectacular, beautifully seductive, and mind-blowing as possible, but that ultimately leaves the viewer feeling somewhat hollow and small.

"Dreamland was originally written as a kind of early 20th Century Coney Island – there was a Dreamland at Coney Island that burned down in 1911 which was historically rooted in the Pleasure Park aesthetic of the earlier Victorian age with all the architectural juxtapositions of the classical and the lurid that characterize that era. But as we developed this contrasting visual language for Vandevere's Dreamland, Tim wanted us to harken further to the defiantly forward-looking World's Fair park aesthetic of the '30s. Once we assumed Vandevere's ability to enlist the finest entertainment designers and marshal all necessary resources to implement innovative building techniques well ahead of their time, some soaringly seductive shapes started to appear in the architectural models we were exploring. The emerging feel of the park is unique to an expressionistic Burton film, I think, melding both emotionally graphic and historically appropriate environments. It's an interesting amalgam of World's Fair optimism and Coney Island hucksterism.

"I think the look of *Dumbo* expands the stylistic language of Tim's films for people familiar with them. He has always striven to communicate to audiences with the clarity of his vision and I think the film will surprise and delight them with the unique world they will visit. It adds a new chapter."

CONCEPT ART:

01 V.A. Vandevere's Dreamland blends early 20th Century Coney Island with the 1930s World's Fair shows.

02 The welcoming entrance to the Medici Brothers Circus – a circus from a simpler era.

03 Production designer Rick Heinrichs designed the Medici Brothers Big Top to be "a little hard on its luck (and) a bit slumped over – but it's certainly trying to put on a good show."

04 "The Medici Brothers Circus troupe is a family, so there's a warmth we wanted to convey," says Heinrichs.

CONCEPT ART:

05 Dumbo swoops over the futuristic, funfair complex that is Dreamland.

06 Conveying the colorful and exciting activity inside Dreamland's Big Top.

07 Heinrichs describes Dreamland as having an "optimistic futurism."

08 "Tim (Burton) wanted us to harken to the defiantly forward-looking World's Fair park aesthetic of the '30s," Heinrichs explains.

06

09

CONCEPT ART:

09 Welcome to Dreamland!
The production design
team tried to make it "as
spectacular, beautifully
seductive, and mind-blowing
as possible," says Heinrichs.

COSTUME DESIGNER

COLLEEN ATWOOD

Dumbo is Oscar-winning costume designer Colleen Atwood's 13th movie with director Tim Burton – and, she admits, he never stops surprising her!

01

02

03

01 Colette Marchant's look was partly inspired by silent movie stars.

02 Colette is "the Lily Langtry of her time," says Colleen Atwood.

03 Atwood surveys her handiwork, with a troupe of Dreamland performers. (Photo: Jay Maidment)

04 The first time we meet Holt Farrier (Colin Farrell), he's still in uniform.

05 Holt, wearing one of his snazzier shirts.

06 "He has a couple of show outfits," Atwood says of Holt, "but mainly he's in work clothes."

Colleen Atwood: "The first step of costume design with a movie like this is reading the screenplay and having a conversation with the director, which in this case is Tim Burton. Once I knew how he saw it, what he was looking for in the story, I began my journey with research into circuses in America during this time period – and circuses in Europe, too, because a lot of the American acts came out of Europe. I think that had a lot to do with how the costumes and the look of the circuses evolved.

"No one has a lot of costumes in the Medici Brothers Circus. Traditionally, circus performers made their own costumes, and the clothes reflect that in the early part of the movie. They're well worn, they're well loved and they're maintained – so I kept it very simple. But when they travel to New York, they get a new kit. They've got a little money in their pockets, and they get new city clothes, because they've finally realized what they think is their dream.

"My big players were Holt, played by Colin Farrell, the children (Nico Parker and Finley Hobbins), Danny DeVito, Michael Keaton, and Eva Green. It's not a big clothes movie for Holt: he comes back from war in a uniform and he has a couple of show outfits, but mainly he's in work clothes. So it's a very humble costuming process with Holt and his children, who wear everyday clothes. But that is accented by huge, glamorous show costumes on the other side of the coin. As Medici, Danny has a suit I call "Purple Rain," because it's all purple, and he has a big, checked suit. There's always a bit of a tacky vibe to his clothes, but with a worn quality.

"Keaton's character, Vandevere, has a certain dash to his costumes. He deals with bankers and he's a bit of a conman, so his suits are very bespoke and showy. With the character of Colette (Eva Green), who is the queen of the air, I took more of a silent-movie stance on her costumes, as well as taking influence from big aerial acts from the period, and circus glamor, which was really fun to do. She's the Lily Langtry of her time.

"On my biggest day, I probably dressed over 200 people as circus acts, with 500 people in the crowd. That was a really big day! It's a big, big show. For the costumes we manufactured, we bought fabric from India, Italy, the UK, and America. So there's an international touch to how things came together.

"I've done many movies with Tim Burton – we've known each other for 20 years, if not more. Every time I work with him, I remember how individual he is. He always surprises me. But the most rewarding part of this job has to be working with the actors and seeing them put on their costumes and become the people they play in the story. All of a sudden you see it in front of you: Danny as Medici, Michael Keaton as Vandevere, Eva Green as the queen of the air. You realize they aren't themselves anymore. They're something else." 𝔇

06

07

08

07 "Vandevere (Michael Keaton) has a certain dash to his costumes," says Atwood.

08 Danny DeVito as Max Medici, in the suit Atwood calls "Purple Rain."

09 Atwood's costume concept designs, which depict a colorful variety of circus performer looks. (Designs: Colleen Atwood, Sketch Artist: Damien Florébert Cuypers)

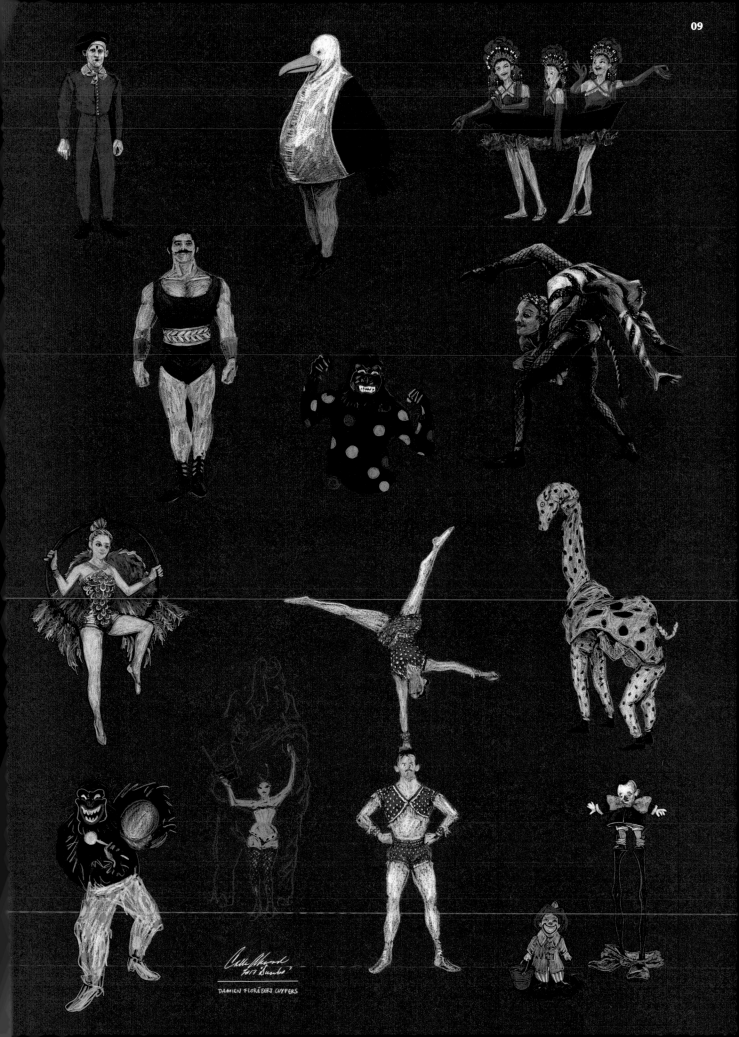

DAMIEN FLORÉBERT CUYPERS

10 Milly (Nico Parker) and Joe (Finley Hobbins) may be circus-raised, but they dress in everyday clothes of the post-World War I era.

11 The brother and sister are united on a quest to reunite Dumbo with his mother.

12 Atwood describes designing the Farrier kids' clothes as "a very humble costuming process."

This concept painting shows V.A. Vandevere
(Michael Keaton) surveying his opulent
show business world, Dreamland. At first it
appears bright and optimistic, but there is
also an emptiness to it.

RICHARD STAMMERS

★ AND ★

HAL COUZENS

Dumbo's visual effects supervisor and visual effects producer detail how they blended reality and magic to bring our ear-flapping hero into a live-action world.

HEAD STUDY A   HEAD STUDY B   HEAD STUDY E   HEAD STUDY D

02

01 Tim Burton directs Eva Green riding a model Dumbo, to be replaced with the digital character during postproduction. (Photo: Jay Maidment)

02 A set of Dumbo head studies. (Photo: Leah Gallo)

03 Visual effects supervisor Richard Stammers adjusts the position of a Dumbo stuffie, while referencing a video feed of the scene. (Photo: Jay Maidment)

04 Practical effects were used as well as digital ones – in this case for a scene in which Mrs. Jumbo showers her baby Dumbo. (Photo: Jay Maidment)

05 A pre-vis (early visual effects) depiction of Dumbo's first flight.

Richard Stammers (visual effects supervisor):
When we first came onboard we knew our main task was going to be creating our hero character for the movie. With no real elephants being used in the film, we had to create a digital version of Dumbo, as well as his mom and the other elephants. We had to figure out his size and the size of his ears, knowing he had to fly and be able to carry people – which was a further step beyond what was in the original animation. Figuring that out was a design challenge. We started with a regular-sized baby elephant, then combined that with ear designs to see how that would work. We also looked at frames from the original cartoon alongside poses of real baby elephants, trying to find that cute similarity between the two. That was an interesting process, but confirmed we needed to steer away from reality for his body proportions and any natural physics of flight for his air-born animation.

Hal Couzens (visual effects producer): Dumbo "lives" in a real world live-action context, so he is subject to physics, despite being able to fly. To aid the illusion, we made his ears slightly bigger when he was in flight, to give him a bigger wingspan, hoping it would seem more believable that he could fly. They couldn't be *too* long on the ground, or they'd get in the way all the time.

Stammers: There is a journey in terms of his growth through the film. His starting point as a small newborn size,

combined with a little clumsiness, gives an adorable look to his performance, but a lot of our work involved building a very emotive face. Much of this was expressed through the eyes, with minimal facial movement, to avoid him looking too cartoony.

Couzens: In story terms, when we reach Dreamland some weeks have passed so we made Dumbo a little bigger, growing from 85 centimeters to the top of his back, to 103 centimeters. Part of the purpose here was to make it look more like he could carry an adult or kids when he flies.

Stammers: Seeing as how we've got a baby Asian elephant who really has ears the size of an adult African elephant, it gave us some clues as to how the ears would fold and flap around as he walks. In terms of the body proportions, the legs are a little bit shorter than a real elephant's, which allows the body to feel fuller. The trunk is shorter, too, which gives him a cuter look. And we very much kept the blue eyes of the original cartoon, which is obviously the biggest change from a real elephant. We tried to find the right balance between an elephant's eyes and something more human, which allowed us to better read Dumbo's emotions.

Couzens: Throughout the film we've given him a little bit of hair, as opposed to his hairless state in the original cartoon, as this helped him to sit in our photography and be more like a real elephant. D

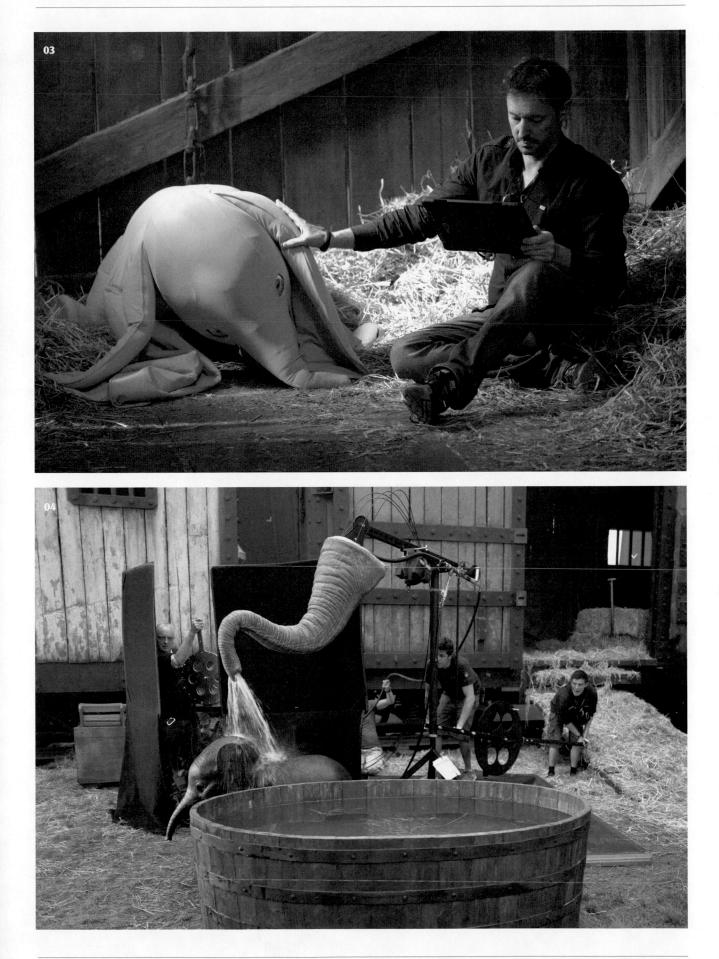

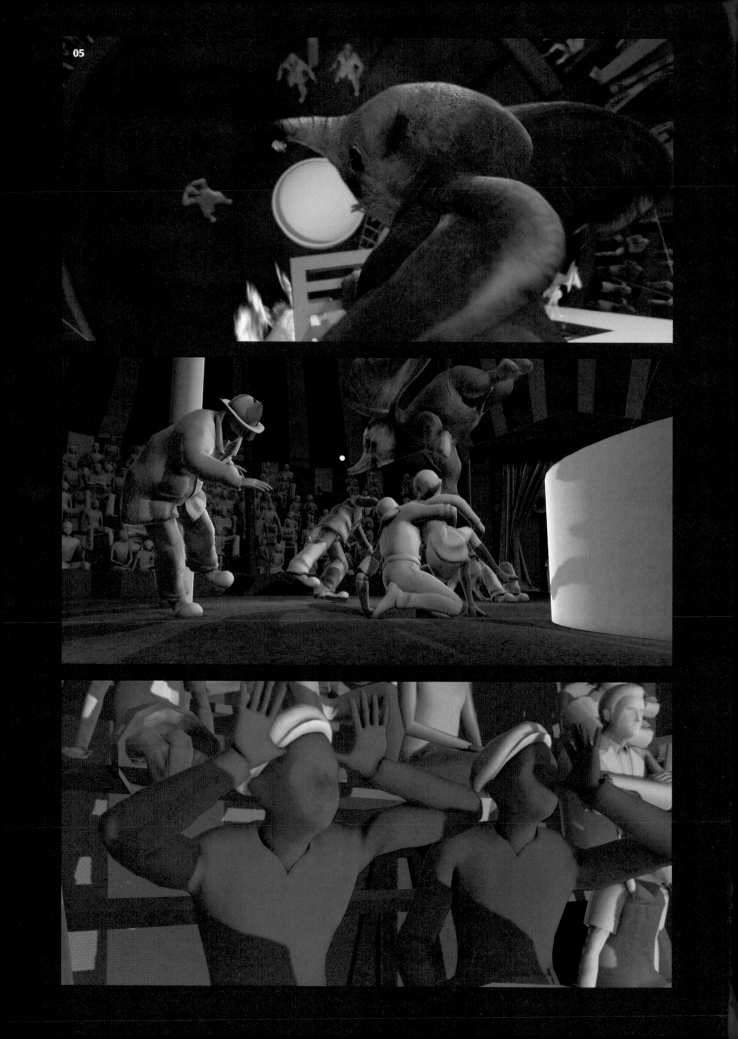

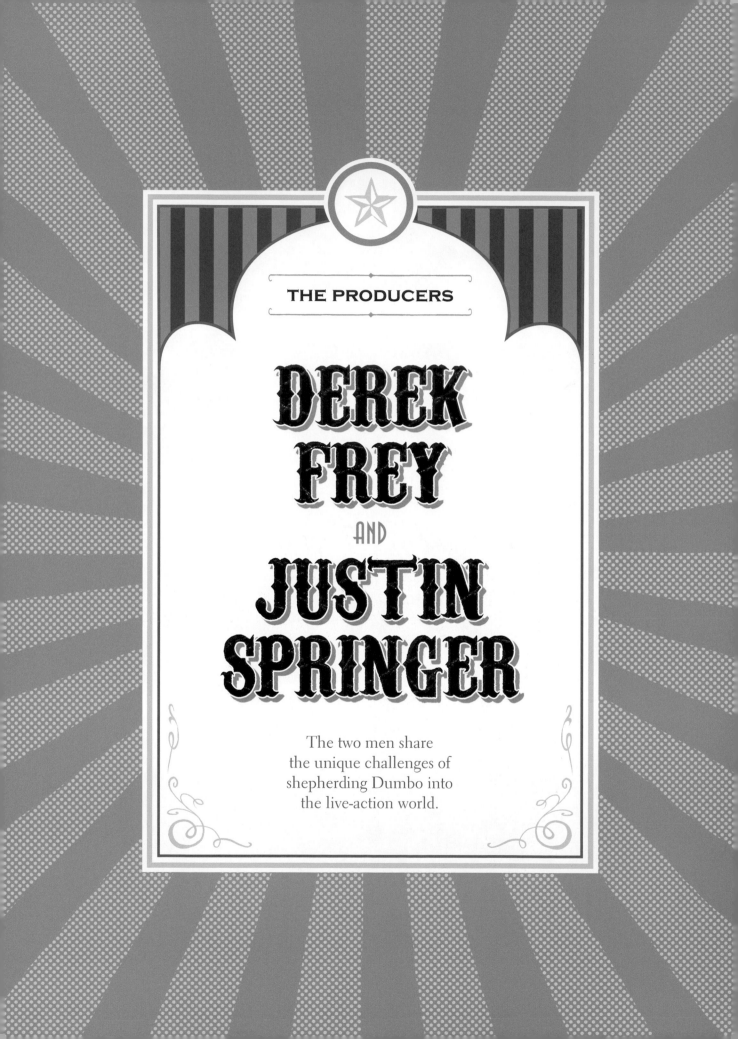

DEREK FREY

AND

JUSTIN SPRINGER

The two men share
the unique challenges of
shepherding Dumbo into
the live-action world.

Dumbo – The Official Movie Special: Why do you think the original *Dumbo* film is still so loved today?

Derek Frey: The image of Dumbo is iconic. All around the world you see that image of the baby elephant with the big ears and people instantly know who he is. They may not remember every single beat of the story, but they remember the tender moments – especially the relationship between Mrs. Jumbo and baby Dumbo.

Justin Springer: It was a very simple story, but also an emotionally poignant one. It's a story about a child and his mother; it's about being different and not fitting in — there is a lot at the core of it that people of all ages can relate to.

Frey: It's something that is ingrained in everyone of all ages, and I think it is the prime time for it to be turned into a live-action movie.

Why is it the right time?

Frey: In this day and age, technology allows you to create animals via the computer and make them look photo-real. It's hard to tell the difference. Ten years ago I don't think you'd be able to achieve the realism you can now, and a lot of films that have come out in recent years – including some Disney films – have proven just how convincingly animals can be recreated.

Why is it such a great choice of movie for Tim Burton to make?

Springer: As a fan of Tim's movies, one thing I've always

> "Tim Burton is amazing at creating a distinctive world of his own amidst the real world. It's familiar but also completely original and more wondrous."
> — *Justin Springer*

noticed is that he often tells stories about outsiders, about characters trying to find a place in their world – and to me, Dumbo is this all-time great outsider character.

Frey: He is the ultimate outsider. One of the first outsiders. And if you're familiar with Tim's work you understand he's built all his stories around outsiders, so it makes perfect sense.

Springer: Also, Tim Burton is amazing at creating a distinctive world of his own amidst the real world, as opposed to a fantasy world. Often his movies take place in our world, but he's able to infuse it with a little bit of magic and his own point of view in a way that makes it familiar but also completely original and more wondrous than the one we know.

Would you describe this as a remake?

Frey: No, this is not a remake. It carries you through a lot of the story points of the original, and you'll see a lot of action that you're maybe familiar with from the ▶

01 The Farrier family (Colin Farrell, Finley Hobbins and Nico Parker), who commit themselves to helping Dumbo.

01

02

02 A nod to the original *Dumbo* movie, in the "Pink Elephants on Parade" dream sequence.

03 Milly and her father (Farrell) take in the futuristic wonders of Dreamland.

animated film, but then we take it beyond that. Once the world discovers that a flying elephant exists, we answer the question: well, what's going to happen now?

Springer: The original was a movie primarily about the way in which the animal community around Dumbo reacted to this creature born with giant ears who could fly. What we thought would be interesting to explore in a retelling is how the human world around him would react to that magical feat – Holt (Colin Farrell) and his two kids, the Medici Brothers Circus, and the world at large in 1919.

How do Milly (Nico Parker) and Joe (Finley Hobbs) form a relationship with Dumbo?

Springer: In a few ways the kids replace the Timothy Q. Mouse character from the original film. Timothy was the mouse who discovered Dumbo's secret, helped him hatch his plan to use his ability to fly to reconnect with his mom, and was his protector. So in our story, Joe and Milly serve that same role. They are excited about this baby elephant. They don't look down on him for the size of his ears, they think he's the cutest thing they've ever seen. Then they realize he has this ability to fly. While everybody else has other, mostly selfish, interests with Dumbo, Milly, and Joe are purely about helping the young elephant get back to his mother.

How did you go about deciding what Dumbo would look like in this film?

Frey: Well, with Dumbo obviously being a recognizable character from the animated film, there is a responsibility. You want to stay pretty close to the design of the original. The jumping-off point was looking at the cels from the original and trying to bring that into the photo-real world. I feel like where we've fallen is somewhere between the design of the original animated Dumbo and real baby elephants in the wild. He has his blue eyes, he has this certain shape and stature and he's super cute. You can't deny a baby elephant its cuteness.

How did you tackle the challenge of representing Dumbo on set, while you were shooting the movie?

Springer: The movie is set in the real world in 1919. As such, we captured as much in camera as absolutely possible. As for Dumbo he was created using CG, but is meant to fit seamlessly into the real world in which he exists. To create him we used a range of techniques on set to get his character into the scenes physically with the actors, and then cutting-edge computer animation to bring him to life. But making him look real is one thing. It's Tim Burton's experience in animation that was essential to turning him into

03

a living, breathing, and emotive character that we care about.

Frey: It was a challenge to make him a presence on set. We wanted to have something the actors could play against, and also to give our visual effects team reference to do the animation later on. There were a number of different things they could play with, from a green stuffy to give size and scale reference, to a highly detailed maquette that was often used for lighting and camera reference. And then we also had a couple of different suits that one of our actors, Edd Osmond, fitted himself into and walked around in on set.

What kind of nods do you have to the original?
Springer: Music is a big one. There is wonderful music in the original *Dumbo* and we found opportunities to integrate it into our film in ways that work in the context of the story.

Frey: With a retelling of such a memorable film, audiences are going to expect to see nods to the original and Tim definitely provides that. But the nods to the original are not really told in a straightforward way. For example, with the "Pink Elephants on Parade" dream sequence, Tim found a way to do it in Dreamland with people making giant bubbles which transform into the shapes of elephants.

What should we most be looking forward to about seeing this film?
Springer: There's something so instantly charming and sweet about seeing that baby elephant with his floppy, oversized ears get his feet under himself for the first time. And then when he takes flight, it's just magical. Also, to see the way Tim Burton has brought the world of 1919 to life – the costumes, the sets, the large-scale circus and amusement park experiences – it all feels both classic and modern at the same time. He's created an idealized and slightly magical version of the past to which I think audiences will enjoy escaping for a few hours.

Frey: When you see this film, you're going to remember everything you love about the original, and it's going to deliver all the greatness and emotion of that film. But it's also going to take you to a whole new level. It really is the greatest show on earth.

> "This is not a remake. You'll see a lot of action that you're maybe familiar with from the animated film, but then we take it beyond that."
> — *Derek Frey* —

This concept art reveals Dreamland's dark side: Nightmare Island. "It's a mysterious place," explains production designer Rick Heinrichs, "where they have the most dangerous beasts in the world, who are almost depicted as malignant gods and demons."

MEDICI
★ BROS. ★
CIRCUS
SOUTH LAKE
AUG 9 – 10
BIGGER THAN EVER SHOW
AMESH ➤
SNAKE CHARMER
THE MAGNIFICENT!
ON STARS
& HOLT ★
WITH
ERTY HORSES!!!
THRILLING
PE TROUPE
EXTRA ORDINARY
STRONGMAN
PIRING FROM HIS CANON!!!
MANCES DAILY
I AND NIGHT
ED ON THE CIRCUS FIELD

SCREENWRITER

EHREN KRUGER

For the blockbuster wordsmith, bringing
this beloved animated classic into the
world of live-action cinema proved to be
a fascinating journey of discovery.

01 Ehren Kruger, on one of *Dumbo*'s deeply detailed sets.

02 Ring of fire: the Farriers (Nico Parker, Colin Farrell and Finley Hobbins) find themselves in a hot spot.

03 Kruger wrote Milly (Nico Parker) as having ambitions in the realm of science, rather than entertainment.

> "*Dumbo* is the simplest of fables and a reminder that the things that make people different are the things that make people special."

Dumbo – The Official Movie Special: **Why did you want to adapt *Dumbo*?**
Ehren Kruger: *Dumbo* was always my favorite Disney animated film and it made me imagine what a joy it would have been to be a part of Dumbo's circus. The original story took place in a human world, and yet its human characters mostly lived in the background. What would it have been like to be one of them, witnessing Dumbo's amazing journey? In an age of live-action adaptations of classic animated stories, it now seemed possible to experience the *Dumbo* tale from a slightly different, parallel perspective. If Dumbo was real, how would he affect the lives of the humans in his circus family – in addition to his fellow animals? That seemed fascinating to explore.

What was it about the original film that resonated with you?
At its essence, *Dumbo* is the simplest of fables: a reminder that the things that make us different are the things that make us special. What others define as our flaws, we can turn into our strengths – and we all have that power within us. That core message is timeless and profound.

Why do you think this story is so widely beloved?
Dumbo is a character who represents innocence, optimism and hope – and despite all the trials life throws at him, his beautiful worldview survives it all. He reminds us of all the times in our lives when we face a seemingly impossible obstacle, yet with help from our friends and belief in ourselves we discover a path to the other side. Dumbo is also a perfect visual representation of an essential truth to human nature: we all feel like freaks most of the time. We all feel flawed, imperfect, damaged. But some inner "mouse" voice also reminds us that those definitions are just illusions. It may take work and trust and courage, but we all have the ability to recognize ourselves – and one another – as unique and magical creatures in this world.

How did you tackle the adaptation, in terms of being respectful to the original?
I didn't want to change the essential story of *Dumbo*. I just wanted to approach it from an angle that made people feel like they were witnessing Dumbo's journey as fellow members of his circus. That was the escapist, wish-fulfillment aspect that seemed to make the story worth revisiting in a live-action tale. And that opened up all kinds of questions about what an elephant's quest to reunite with his family would mean to the humans in that circus – how it might affect their own ideas of family, justice, fame and self-belief. In addition, I felt there might be a bit more to Dumbo's journey than the original animated film had time to tell. At a short 64 minutes, it ends at the height of Dumbo's fame, with his "super power" secret now known to the world, and I couldn't help wondering – what happens to him *then*?

The human family at the heart of this story is the Farrier family: Holt, Milly, and Joe. What can you tell us about them?
Holt Farrier is a one-time circus star who went off to serve in World War I. When the story opens, he returns as a

03

changed and damaged man, unable to be the star circus attraction he was before. As a last resort, he accepts a job as an elephant trainer, but it's a challenge for Holt and his children Milly and Joe (Nico Parker and Finley Hobbins) to connect as a family the same way they did before. In addition, their little circus is struggling, and the strain is felt by everyone – especially Milly. She's been raised in a circus her entire life but has never truly felt like that's where she belongs. Her interests lie in science and invention, not spectacle and showmanship, and she's struggling to find a place where she fits in.

What can you tell us about Dumbo and his mother, Mrs. Jumbo?

As in the animated film, the story opens with Dumbo born to his loving mother, a circus elephant known as Mrs. Jumbo, who performs with the small-time Medici Brothers Circus. Its owner, Max Medici (Danny DeVito), hopes that a cute baby elephant will prove an enticing new attraction. However, Mrs. Jumbo ends up blamed ▶

THE WRITE WAY

THREE EHREN KRUGER SCRIPTS THAT PAVED HIS PATH TO *DUMBO*

ARLINGTON ROAD (1999)
This taut, twisted mystery thriller was Kruger's breakthrough script, which proved he could match intricate plotting with detailed character work. Jeff Bridges starred as a man who begins to suspect his friendly neighbors (played by Tim Robbins and Joan Cusack) might be terrorist bombers.

TRANSFORMERS: REVENGE OF THE FALLEN (2009)
The first of three *Transformers* sequels Kruger worked on, which required

balancing a relatable human element (primarily in the form of Shia LaBeouf's Sam Witwicky) with a visual-effects driven spectacular. And blockbusters didn't come much bigger and brasher than the *Transformers* films.

GHOST IN THE SHELL (2017)
Dumbo isn't the first time Kruger has adapted an animated movie – he turned Japanese anime classic *Ghost in the Shell* into a bold live-action thriller which starred Scarlett Johansson as a cybernetically enhanced super-agent.

for a tragic accident and is sold away to parts unknown. A devastated Dumbo doesn't know if he'll ever see her again. Then with help from Milly and Joe, he discovers his aerial talents, and the trio realize they may be able to use Dumbo's magic to work toward a reunion with his mom.

What nods are there to the original film in this version of *Dumbo*?

There are lots of scenes and shots and production design details that are nods and homages to the animated classic. Given that a human perspective really shapes this telling, the Timothy Q. Mouse character takes a more minor role, but he's there. We wanted to keep as much of the music from the original film as felt warranted, too: the classic "Baby Mine" song, "Casey Junior" and "Pink Elephants on Parade." Our hope is that this movie feels like it runs on a parallel train track with the animated original, with events that were once seen from the perspective of animals, here experienced from the slightly different perspective of people.

Why did you decide to replace Timothy Q. Mouse with the children?

It was critical to me that the circus world feel as realistic as possible, so at the outset we made the decision not to feature any talking animals. This felt like a very organic trade because Dumbo himself never speaks in the original, and Mrs. Jumbo gets perhaps a line or two. Dumbo was always portrayed through expression and behavior, like a great silent film actor like Charlie Chaplin or Buster Keaton. Again, I was less interested in "remaking" the original movie line-for-line and more interested in what Dumbo's tale might look like from an adjusted angle. So instead of a chorus of animals, we sought to create a menagerie of human characters with their own relationships to Dumbo, and for whom

> "I was surprised at how much of the early circus industry was based on con artistry — trying to convince people there were magical animals and creatures and oddities. It was all a con job!"

06

Dumbo's journey might ultimately affect the ways they see themselves. The mouse character of Timothy was by and large replaced by Holt's children: Milly and Joe. They are the small but mighty optimists who here become Dumbo's greatest champions. In fact, in early drafts of the script, the children were named Tim and Milly – a bit of a bifurcation of "Timothy."

What do you think it was about the script that attracted Tim Burton to direct?

I think, firstly, the original *Dumbo* was a movie that was quite meaningful for him. He felt a kinship for the character and his journey, as well as the artistry and beauty of the animation itself. As a filmmaker, he's often been drawn to the stories of characters whom society perceives as outsiders and oddballs – from Pee-Wee to Edward Scissorhands to Batman – and *Dumbo* is a classic example of that. I think he was also inspired by the challenge of depicting a digitally drawn hero through pure expression and movement – as if he were the throwback star of a silent film. And while Tim doesn't consider himself a "circus aficionado," he certainly is a storyteller who enjoys spending time with misfit families, which describes most of the families I know.

What kind of research did you do, to put this circus world together?

I put a lot of research into the "Golden Age" of the circus, the seismic changes to the entertainment business happening in early 20th Century America, and the history of Coney Island. For a long time I'd wanted to write a movie that took place there, so I asked myself, "If Dumbo were real, what's the biggest stage he would have appeared on?" I knew a story set in 1919 would have to end up in New York City, on the boardwalk of Coney Island, which was really the Las Vegas of its day.

Did anything surprise you while you were doing your research?

I was surprised by how much of the early circus industry was the province of con artists, crooks, and snake oil salesman – doing their level best to convince the world that their "magical" creatures, oddities, and freaks were real. That's why I got so excited about the notion of this historical backdrop for the *Dumbo* story. How would the characters of this world – some of them noble, some nefarious – react to actual magic in their midst?

What excites you most about the way Tim Burton has visualized this?

Watching Dumbo's world come to life under Tim's direction truly makes me feel like I've been transported back to the golden age of the circus. Sometimes going to the right movie feels like climbing into a time machine, and I really feel like Tim has crafted one of those blissful experiences.

What has most impressed you about the cast of this movie?

They've all brought wonderful gravity and emotion to their characters, as well as lots of humor, and I find them completely endearing and believable as a struggling circus family. Plus, the difficulty of acting opposite an invisible magic elephant who is inevitably going to upstage them all cannot be overstated – and they've all been good sports about that!

What do you think will most impress audiences?

You're going to be transported back to the golden age of the circus and you'll come to believe that the impossible's possible. You're going to see an elephant fly, and you're going to feel that – once upon a time, circa 1919 – that little elephant named Dumbo was real. 🎬

04 Milly (Parker) next to her mouse circus. She and Joe (Hobbins) replace the role of the original's Timothy Q. Mouse in this movie.

05 The Medici Brothers Circus in full swing. Kruger did deep research into real circuses of the period while writing the script.

06 Concept art for Dumbo's emotional farewell.

"When you see *Dumbo* you're going to remember everything you love about the original. But it's also going to take you to a whole new level. It really is the greatest show on Earth."

— Derek Frey, producer